Carrying the Light from My Grandparents
Martin Luther King, Jr., and **Coretta Scott King**

We Dream a World

by
Yolanda Renee King

illustrated by
Nicole Tadgell

Orchard Books
an Imprint of Scholastic Inc.
New York

Granddaddy and Grandma . . .

You had a dream we would be judged by what's in our hearts, not by the color of our skin.

You were gone before I came
into this world, but that dream —
and so many others — lives deep
inside me.

Everything you believed in still
shines like the brightest sunrise
on a golden horizon.

Many ask me:

Do you plan to follow in Dr. King and Coretta Scott King's footsteps?

How will you ever fill their shoes?

Do you have what it takes to walk their path?

I hold fast to all that
you stood for —
peace,
togetherness,
harmony,
and love.

Granddaddy and Grandma, thanks to your wisdom
and determination, I now have my own footsteps,
my own journey. My own dreams for our world.

And so, while I **follow** your example,
I am also ready to **lead**.

I Am Ready to walk the uncertain road from today to tomorrow.

I Am Ready to keep my eyes on the prize that you set out before us with the power of your vision.

Yes, Grandma Coretta!
Yes, Granddaddy Martin!

I. Am. Ready.

Every day, I thank you for the gifts you gave so many of us through your hard work.

Because of you, I know that struggle and triumph are bigger than just **me**.

The promise of a new day starts with **me**.

You helped us **see** the dream.

Now we're here to **be** the dream.

The wisdom of your words weaves
a rainbow that lights our way.

Grandaddy, you told us: "**LOVE** is the key."

Grandma, you taught us: "When the heart is right, the mind and body will follow."

These words — these keys to **our** hearts — opened the door to all that is possible.

My parents remind me that in your lives together you shared what came to be called a "revolution of values."

I'm sorry there are still so many problems to endure.
You devoted **your** lives to making **our** lives better.

And now it's my turn to start a new revolution that values kindness, truth, equality, and service.

There are still rocks in the road.

I wish you were here so we could walk it together.

Because our dreams need the strength of a love so powerful that nothing can stop them — or us.

We Dream a World
where school is a safe place, free of fear.

No violence spoken here.

We Dream a World
where guns are not games.

Shoot for the stars, not at each other.

We Dream a World
where poverty is a memory.

Liberty,
justice,
and food for all.

We Dream a World where the only walls are those that hold safe spaces, and have windows and mirrors that reflect our unity.

Beauty has no boundaries.

We Dream a World where trees, flowers, and the earth's creatures thrive in their right seasons.

Spring, summer, winter, fall.
Honesty is the warmest climate.

We Dream a World where bullies turn their backs on being mean.

Let kindness begin with me.

We Dream a World where sickness can be driven out by the healing power of hope.

Love is the cure.

We Dream a World where every child can go to college.

Education fuels our nation.

Reading is believing.

Grandma and Granddaddy, so
many want to know:

**How will you honor your
grandparents' legacy?**

The answer is simple.

We keep *your* dream alive by planting
our dreams, like trees in an orchard,
to be nurtured by tomorrow's gardeners.

With determined feet
blazing a new path . . .

We Are Ready
to take the torch you lit
before we were born.

We Are Ready
to grip that glistening baton.

To hold faith by the hand.

To pass it on.

We Are Ready to reach!

To rise!

To sparkle like stars in a bold blue sky.

Our time has come to bring our twinkle,
letting everyone know:

**Spread the word!
Have you heard?**

All across the nation,
We are going to be
A great generation!

From today to tomorrow,

We
Dream
a World

A Word from Yolanda's Parents, Martin Luther King III and Arndrea Waters King

We've raised our daughter to be strong and independent. As the granddaughter of Martin Luther King, Jr., and Coretta Scott King, Yolanda has grown up surrounded by a legacy of civil rights. From the time she was very young, she's been a girl who cares deeply about equality, harmony, fairness, and helping others. We instilled in our only child the values of her beloved grandparents. We've also encouraged Yolanda's big dreams for our world's future, while at the same time keeping her grounded in the day-to-day realities of what it means to be a young activist and how to inspire others through words and actions.

On March 24, 2018, we attended the March For Our Lives, a demonstration led by students seeking legislation to prevent gun violence. The rally was held in Washington, DC. Turnout across the United States was estimated between 1.2 and 2 million people, making it one of the biggest protests in American history!

We attended the protest in Washington as a family so we could witness and support the aspirations of young people. Though stopping gun violence is one of the issues Yolanda is very passionate about, she hadn't planned to speak at the event. In a sudden, unexpected moment, Yolanda was invited to address the crowd! As any parents might be, we were a bit apprehensive about the magnitude of it all, and we were uncertain about seeing our daughter thrust into such a bright spotlight. But Yolanda was eager and ready — and not the least bit nervous. She reminded us, and everyone who heard her words, that young people can have a voice, and that we adults need to let them speak. The presence and conviction of so many children at that rally was proof that children from all walks of life, and from many kinds of families, have a stake in our future.

The King family finds connection by visiting places important to their family's history, including the Martin Luther King, Jr., memorial monument in Washington, DC (above) and Atlanta's Ebenezer Baptist Church, where Martin Luther King, Jr., served as pastor (below).

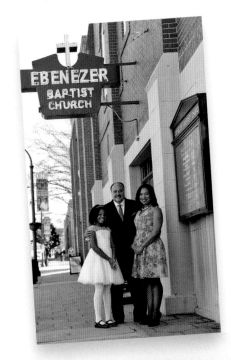

Yolanda inspires young activists to reach for the greatest heights through public speaking and writing.

As parents, we want what all parents would like for their children — health, safety, joy, and the promise of a bright tomorrow. We talk to our daughter about the important role she plays in shaping her future, and the ways in which young people can bring about change. Yolanda talks to us about how and why even small, simple acts of compassion can have a powerful impact, and that any child can become an activist by simply being kind. When Yolanda told us that she wanted to write a book that pays tribute to her grand-parents, we were very pleased to know that her words and the values of the King family would become a book that all families can enjoy together and that can foster important conversations among adults and children at home, school, and the larger community. *We Dream a World* draws its inspiration from Langston Hughes's poem entitled "I Dream a World," a narrative that is a favorite among the books in our home library. We hope you'll enjoy *We Dream a World* with the young people in your lives, and that you'll share it with generations to come.

Martin Luther King III
and Arndrea Waters King

Painting Legacy

I am proud to be a part of empowering the young people who will read this book. As an African American woman, the strength and passion of Yolanda Renee King's words lifted me up with inspiration and hope. Pictures in my head of children — all ages, ethnicities, complexions, orientations, and abilities — came instantly. I envisioned children at work and at play: shy, bold, differently abled, collaborating, expressing themselves in creative ways.

As the illustrator of more than thirty books, I'm still in love with the expressive nature of watercolor painting. In the art, I rendered images of Reverend Dr. Martin Luther King, Jr., and Coretta Scott King using warm tones to convey sepia-hued images of the past. Imaginative and inspirational color combinations drift from one page to another, melding past and present. My goal was to connect elements and themes between page spreads to fit hand in hand with Yolanda's words. My images are symbolic and metaphorical, rather than literal.

Young readers may see themselves reflected in these paintings, becoming even more open-minded, inspired, and passionate to make a difference, just as Yolanda Renee King knows they can be. May they discover that making an impact in the world need not wait for adulthood.

Nicole Tadgell

About Yolanda's Inspiration

Yolanda Renee King never met her grandfather, Dr. Martin Luther King, Jr. But the young activist is one of the countless changemakers inspired by his actions. Dr. King helped change the course of history by spreading a message of equality for all people, regardless of their race or color.

To many, Yolanda's grandfather is the face of the civil rights movement of the 1950s and 1960s. Back then, segregation was a way of life in many parts of the United States, especially in the South. That meant Black people were not allowed to attend the same schools, get treated in the same hospitals, or even use the same drinking fountains as White people. Also, laws in some states kept many Black people from voting, and a lot of businesses refused to hire Black workers.

Dr. King organized peaceful protests to demand equal rights for African Americans and to try to end unjust laws. His powerful speeches inspired many others to join the cause. Sadly, Dr. King was shot and killed in 1968. His birthday is celebrated in one hundred countries across the globe. Dr. King's legacy lives on through the hearts and actions of millions, who, like Yolanda, keep the torch of hope alive by dreaming of a better world.

The strength and resilience of Yolanda's grandparents and civil rights crusaders such as Congressman John Lewis (pictured with the King family in front of the Edmund Pettus Bridge) live on through the next generation of trailblazers.

For my grandparents, Papa King,
Gaga King, Gaga, and Papa.

– YRK

For Grant and Claire.

– NT

Library of Congress Cataloging-in-Publication Data Available
ISBN 978-1-338-75397-4
10 9 8 7 6 5 4 3 2 1   24 25 26 27 28
Printed in China   38
First edition, January 2024
Book design by Doan Buu and Patti Ann Harris
The text and display type were set in Neutraface Text.
The illustrations were created traditionally using Winsor-Newton watercolors, fabriano artistico hot press paper, graphite
and edited with Adobe Photoshop.